LAW & JUSTICE

by

Charlie Ogden

©2017
Book Life
King's Lynn
Norfolk PE30 4LS

Written by:
Charlie Ogden

Edited by:
Grace Jones

ISBN: 978-1-78637-142-3

Designed by:
Natalie Carr

All rights reserved
Printed in Malaysia

A catalogue record for this book
is available from the British Library.

Photocredits
Abbreviations: l–left, r–right, b–bottom, t–top, c–centre, m–middle.

Front Cover t – Orhan Cam. Front Cover b – ER_09. 2 – Andrey Burmakin. 4 – wavebreakmedia. 5tr – SergeBertasiusPhotography. 5ml – StacieStauffSmith Photos. 5mr – Nagel Photography. 5bl – View Apart. 6 – corgarashu. 7 – Jacob Lund. 8tr – Katiekk. 8bl – l i g h t p o e t. 9 – Joseph Sohm. 10br – Ditty_about_summer. 11 – By Unknown or not provided (U.S. National Archives and Records Administration) [Public domain], via Wikimedia Commons. 12tr – Stuart Monk. 12bl – andras_csontos. 13tr – Andrey_Popov. 13bl – OFFFSTOCK. 14 – Yorkman. 15 – Monkey Business Images. 16 – Ronnachai Palas. 17 – UTBP. 18l – Konstantin Shevtsov. 18l – Byelikova Oksana. 18m – Filipe Frazao. 18r – Kobby Dagan. 18r – Joel Shawn. 19 – thomas koch. 20 – Paul Wishart. 21tl – bikeriderlondon. 21mr – bikeriderlondon. 21bl – wavebreakmedia. 22 – Marbury. 23 – jsp. 24 – BortN66 . 25 – By Jack Delano, photographer [Public domain], via Wikimedia Commons 26 _ bikeriderlondon. 27 – superoke. 28 – Niran Phonruang. 30 – Andrey_Popov.

Images are courtesy of Shutterstock.com, unless stated otherwise. With thanks to Getty Images, Thinkstock Photo and iStockphoto.

CONTENTS

Words in **bold** can be found in the glossary on page 31.

WHAT ARE LAWS?

Every country in the world has their own set of laws. Laws are rules that are put in place by a country's **government**. They apply to everyone **equally** and everyone must follow them.

A person who does not follow the law is committing a **crime** and will usually be punished. As their punishment, they might be sent to prison, forced to pay money to the government or made to work within the **community** for free.

The reason that laws exist is to help communities to become places where everyone can live together happily. They are supposed to help communities to be **moral**, safe and fair. There are four main ways that laws do this.

A COUNTRY'S GOVERNMENT IS USUALLY ABLE TO CHANGE LAWS, GET RID OF OLD LAWS AND MAKE NEW LAWS.

LAW REPORTS 171   172   173   174   175   176

THE PURPOSES OF LAWS

Laws help to stop people from doing **immoral** things by by explaining which actions are good and which are bad. For example, the law says that stealing is wrong. Laws also allow people to be **legally** stopped from doing bad things, which is usually done by the police.

Laws help to make a community work together. They cause people to organise themselves into doing things that will help everyone. For example, laws that stop people from throwing rubbish into rivers, lakes or onto the street help to protect nature and keep a community clean.

Laws provide a way for people to settle arguments **peacefully**. If there were no laws, a person might take it upon themselves to punish others who they thought had done something wrong. Instead, they can take those people to **court**.

Laws make it so that people can be punished for doing things that are wrong. This makes a community fairer as people can't benefit from doing bad things. Many people also think that people who break the law and hurt people deserve to be punished.

WHAT IS JUSTICE?

The idea of justice relates to fairness, being moral and people getting what they deserve. When people talk about justice, they often talk about someone getting what they deserved after performing certain actions. For example, if your friend was being bullied by someone and then the bully got told off for it, you could say that this was justice. However, justice can relate to many more things, such as helping someone who has been harmed or sharing things out fairly.

When a certain event or action is seen as justice, it is said to be just. When a certain event or action isn't seen as justice; for example, if your friend got told off instead of the bully; it is said to be unjust.

Weighing scales are often used as a **symbol** of justice. They show how opinions and facts need to be weighed up and carefully thought about before justice can be achieved.

When people talk about justice, a lot of the time they only talk about punishing people. A common example of justice is someone being sent to prison after stealing money. Even though this is an example of justice, as it could be argued that the person got what they deserved for stealing, this is not the only kind of justice.

While people often believe that those who commit crimes deserve punishment, others believe that people who act morally or do good things deserve rewards. Because of this, rewarding those people who deserve it can also be thought of as justice. For example, if a person worked very hard at their job for a long time, you could say that giving them a promotion would be the just thing to do.

LAW AND JUSTICE

Some people would argue that in a perfect world everyone would get what they deserved – there would be perfect justice. People would be fairly punished for the bad things that they did and others would be fairly rewarded for the good things that they did. Everyone who stole something would be punished and everyone who worked hard and acted morally would be rewarded.

From this look at a perfectly just **society**, we can learn something about justice – it should be universal. If something is universal it means that it applies equally to everyone everywhere. Most people would agree that if a doctor in France and a shoe salesman in Sudan both stole the same amount of money, then they should be punished equally. This is because most people believe that justice should be universal and should be applied equally to everyone, no matter where they live or what job they have.

A country's laws are also universal, meaning that they are equally applied to everyone in that country. Because of this, laws can help to give people justice.

Laws help to give people justice by working out what punishments and rewards are fair and equal. Even if everyone agrees that the French doctor and the Sudanese shoe salesman should both be punished, we need to work out how they can be punished in a fair and equal way. Today, we use laws to work out what a person's punishment should be. Laws give us a way to work out fair and just punishments for people so that justice can be universal.

There is a very strong link in today's world between the law and justice, making many people think that we could not have justice without the law.

EQUAL · JUSTICE · UNDER · LAW ·

LAW AND INJUSTICE

While it may be true that societies could never be just without laws, it is certainly true that societies are not always just even when they do have laws.

One reason that societies with laws aren't always just is because laws aren't truly universal. While everyone in one country is equally affected by their laws, people in other countries follow different laws. Because of this, it is very unlikely that a French doctor and a Sudanese shoe salesman would be punished equally, even if they stole exactly the same amount of money.

- ■ No data
- ■ No minimum age
- ■ 9–13 years old
- ■ 14–15 years old
- ■ 16–17 years old
- ■ 18 years or older

This map shows how old you have to be in each country before you can get legally married. This shows that laws are different in different countries, which means that laws aren't truly universal.

In France, people usually have to pay a **fine** or spend time in prison if they steal. However, in Sudan you can have your hand cut off for stealing. As justice is universal and should be equal for everyone, we know that these punishments cannot both be just, even though they are both based on laws. This shows that sometimes the law does not always lead to justice.

The jungles in Vietnam were a very dangerous and scary place to fight a war.

Another way to see that laws don't always result in justice is by looking at what laws relate to. In most cases, laws only talk about what actions are **illegal** and how people should be punished if they do illegal things. However, justice isn't only about punishing illegal actions. Sometimes being kind and generous is the just thing to do.

After the Vietnam War ended in 1975, thousands of American soldiers went back to America. For years they had been far away from their homes and fighting in a horrible war. Many people agree that it would have been just

for the American **public** to help these soldiers when they got back to America. However, many people hated the soldiers and treated them very badly because they thought that America shouldn't have been in the war. The soldiers found it hard to find jobs and many of them ended up homeless with no one helping them.

Today, many people agree that not helping these soldiers was unjust. However, it wasn't illegal because the law doesn't usually talk about situations where being kind is the just thing to do.

TYPES OF JUSTICE

DISTRIBUTIVE JUSTICE

This relates to what people get back from their community. People around the world give money to their governments so that they can provide things like roads, schools and police officers. This is called paying taxes. Because everyone pays money into their community, it is only fair that they get something back from their community as well. The benefits of living in a community, such as going to school and being protected by the police, should be equally and fairly given out to all members of the community.

> THERE ARE FOUR MAIN TYPES OF JUSTICE.

PROCEDURAL JUSTICE

Procedural justice relates to whether rules and laws are fairly applied to different people. Rules that need to be fairly applied are rules that don't always apply to everyone equally. For example, if a baby took a chocolate bar from a shop, it wouldn't be fair to punish them for stealing because babies don't know what stealing is.

RESTORATIVE JUSTICE

This type of justice relates to helping people who have been unjustly hurt in some way. For example, people who have had loved ones die in war often get help from the government as a form of restorative justice. This type of justice also relates to people getting what they deserve after working hard. If a person works very hard at their job and deserves a promotion, then not giving them that promotion could harm them because they might feel as if they've wasted their efforts. Because of this, giving them the promotion is a form of restorative justice.

RETRIBUTIVE JUSTICE

This is the type of justice that usually comes to mind when people think about justice; it relates to punishing people who have acted in immoral ways or hurt people. Retributive justice states that people who have hurt others in some way should have to give up something. Usually people are forced to give up their **freedom** by being sent to prison. However, for a person's punishment to count as restorative justice it must be equal to the harm that they have caused. For example, sending someone to prison for swearing would not count as restorative justice as the punishment is too strict.

JUSTICE AND HUMAN RIGHTS

Human rights are things that everyone should be able to do simply because they are human. Rights are things that you can do because of who you are – for example, police officers have the right to drive police cars. Human rights are things that you have the right to do just because you are a human! Not everyone agrees on what is and what is not a human right, but there are a few human rights that nearly everyone agrees on. These include the right to equality, the right to a fair **trial** and the right to **liberty**.

Many people believe that the right to justice is an important human right. This human right says that everyone has the right to live in a community where people can be brought to justice. Part of this human right includes the right to be protected by a police force who will punish people in the community who hurt others or act immorally.

JUSTICE AND EQUALITY

Another important human right is the right to equality. This human right says that every person has the right to live in a society that promotes the equality of all people. Such a society would view everyone as equally important, give everyone the same rights and allow everyone the same opportunities.

Many people believe that, for justice to be achieved, everyone has to be treated equally. As justice is universal, two people who commit the same crime should be punished in the same way or with equal severity. This could mean that they go to prison for the same amount of time. However, if two people were not seen as equal, meaning that they did not have their right to equality, then they might not be sent to prison for the same amount of time. If this happened, it would be unjust. Because of this, some people think that the right to equality is more important than the right to justice, because people have to be treated equally before they can be treated in a just way.

JUSTICE AND FAIR TRIALS

Many people agree that the right to a fair trial is an important human right. This right means that every person can defend themselves and try to prove their innocence in a court before they are punished for doing something illegal. This is an important human right as sometimes people are **accused** of doing things that they never actually did.

Every year, people are sent to prison for crimes that they did not commit because their country's government does not allow them the right to a fair trial.

The right to a fair trial and the right to justice are very closely linked. The right to justice is all about people getting what they deserve for the actions they've performed. The right to a fair trial is all about people having a fair chance to prove what actions they have or have not performed. If people do not have the right to a fair trial, then people will not have a chance to prove that they did nothing wrong. This would mean that people could get punished for things that they never did, which is certainly unjust. Because of this, most people believe that you need to have the right to a fair trial before you can have the right to justice.

JUSTICE AND LIBERTY

The right to liberty is often seen as the most important human right. 'Liberty' means freedom, so the right to liberty means that everyone should be free to choose where they live, how they dress and what they eat. It says that every person has the right to choose how they live their life.

The Statue of Liberty in America is a symbol for the liberty and freedom of the American people.

Even though many people say that the right to liberty is the most important human right, it seems that sometimes the right to justice comes first. The right to justice involves retributive justice, which says that people who have done immoral things or hurt people should have to give up something. In a lot of cases, this means that a person goes to prison. In prison, people do not get to choose where they live, what they eat or how they dress, showing that prisoners do not have freedom or their right to liberty. This shows that the right to justice sometimes comes first and can lead to other human rights, like the right to liberty, being taken away.

DECIDING WHAT IS JUST

The most difficult part of maintaining the right to justice is working out what actually is the most just thing to do. The only thing that we know about justice so far is that it should be universal. What is just and unjust should be the same everywhere and everyone should be rewarded and punished equally for the just and unjust things that they do.

It is very common for people from different countries to have different ideas, often about such things as food, music and fashion.

Although we know that this is how justice should be, we also know that this is not actually the case in the world. People from different countries have different ideas about what actions are just and what actions are unjust.

As well as this, people from different countries often punish unjust acts and reward just acts in different ways. This can make it very difficult to know what is just and what is unjust.

REFUGEES

Restorative justice is about helping people who have been unfairly harmed. A lot of people think that if they do nothing, then it is impossible for them to be unjust. This is wrong – sometimes doing nothing and not helping is unjust. If your friend really needed help after falling over, lots of people would see it as unjust if you did not help. We can see that people have different views about restorative justice by looking at refugees. Refugees are people who leave their country because they are scared that they will get attacked or killed, often because there is a war going on. Refugees usually have no part in the war and are just trying to protect themselves and their families. Lots of people around the world believe that helping refugees is a form of restorative justice; that helping is the just thing to do and that not helping is unjust. However, there are also lots of people who believe that not helping refugees is not unjust because it is not their fault that the refugees are in trouble. This shows how people often have different views about justice.

Refugees often struggle to find homes, jobs or even clothes.

LEGAL SYSTEMS

People usually decide what is just by using a legal system. A legal system is the process used to work out whether laws have been broken and, if they have, what a just **consequence** would be. Many people believe that legal systems do not always achieve justice, however most people believe that they are the fairest and best way to try to achieve justice. One of the most important parts of any legal system is court. Courts are groups of people who help to work out whether a law has been broken. After this, they help to work out the fairest and most just consequences, whether that would be sending someone to prison or helping the **victims** of a crime.

WHEN A PERSON OR A GROUP OF PEOPLE IS TAKEN TO COURT, IT IS CALLED A 'COURT CASE'.

In many countries, courts are used to settle any argument that is to do with the law. This is how the right to a fair trial is maintained in many places. If a person is accused of committing a crime, going to court gives that person a chance to prove that they did not commit the crime.

Bow Street Magistrates' Court, London, England

BOW STREET MAGISTRATES COURT

Every court case has a plaintiff and a defendant. The plaintiff is the person who is accusing someone of breaking the law. In many cases, the plaintiff is the state. The defendant is the person who has been accused. However, there are lots of other people in courts, all of which have their own job to do.

In most countries, a judge is in charge of the court and makes sure that things happen as they should. The judge usually makes the final decision about what the defendant's punishment will be if they are found to be **guilty**.

Many courts use juries to decide whether a law has been broken. A jury is a group of people from the public who come to court in order to listen to both sides of the argument and work out which side is correct.

There are also lawyers in most courts. Lawyers are people who practise the law and both the plaintiff and the defendant will usually have lawyers in court to help them. When a lawyer helps someone in court, they are said to 'represent' them. Lawyers can only represent either the defendant or the plaintiff, never both.

UNJUST LAWS IN THE PAST

Even though courts today might not always achieve justice, they are still the fairest and most equal method we have to decide whether a law has been broken. By using trained professionals, like lawyers and judges, as well as a jury of people chosen from the public, courts are able to fairly decide whether someone has committed a crime and what a just punishment would be.

In the past, things were not so fair and just. The methods used to decide if a law had been broken were often not fair at all and many of the punishments people were given were not just. For much of history, one person alone would have decided if a crime had been committed, usually a king or some other leader. This made it easier for unjust laws and punishments to be carried out.

HAMMURABI

One of the world's oldest legal systems is called the code of Hammurabi. It was created by King Hammurabi, who lived over 3,500 years ago, and it includes 282 laws. The code explains how much certain people should be paid for doing their job, such as farmers and doctors. As well as this, it also explains things like how much money a builder should give to a person if he built a house for them that then fell down. However, other parts of the code show just how unfair and unjust laws could be in the past.

This is the original code of Hammurabi. It was carved into a large rock over 3,500 years ago. The rock, which is known as a **stela**, is over 2 metres tall and is shaped like a human finger.

The code of Hammurabi is based around the idea that the punishment should fit the crime, meaning that the punishment for a crime should be similar to the crime itself. This is where the saying 'an eye for an eye' came from. Under the code of Hammurabi, if you caused someone to lose their eye, you lost one of your eyes as punishment.

The idea that the punishment should fit the crime is one that most societies gave up on a long time ago because it is not just. One way to show this is by looking at accidents. If you accidentally ripped someone's shirt, the most just thing to do would either be to try to repair the shirt or to buy that person a new shirt. The most just thing to do would not be to rip your own shirt. This is because accidents usually call for restorative justice, not retributive justice.

Another way in which the code of Hammurabi was not just is that it did not see all people as equal. For example, the code mostly only applied to men as women were not seen to be as important. This meant that only men could be the victims of crimes, which led to some very unusual punishments. For example, if Max killed Ben's daughter, Ben would be seen as the victim of the crime, not his daughter. The punishment for Max would then be that his own daughter would have to be killed, even though she did nothing wrong. This is because the punishment had to fit the crime.

JIM CROW LAWS

There are also many examples of unjust laws from more recent times. The Jim Crow Laws, which stayed in place in the Southern United States until 1965, made it so that black people and white people could not use the same services provided by the government. This included things like schools, buses and toilets. This alone shows that these laws were unjust, as people were not being seen as equal. However, it gets worse as these laws show that the government did not respect distributive justice.

While the Jim Crow Laws were in place, black people had to use different schools, buses and toilets to white people. However, the services that black people were allowed to use were much worse than those used by white people. The schools were dirty and had very few books and only old desks and chairs. This shows that the government in the United States of America at the time did not equally share out the benefits of their community. Instead, they gave more to the white people. This was unequal, unfair and unjust.

INJUSTICE AROUND THE WORLD

Nowadays, legal systems are much more just than they were in the past. However, there are still many examples of injustice in the world.

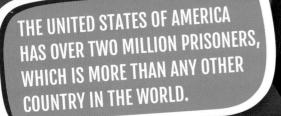

THE UNITED STATES OF AMERICA HAS OVER TWO MILLION PRISONERS, WHICH IS MORE THAN ANY OTHER COUNTRY IN THE WORLD.

The flag of The United States of America

PRISONS IN THE UNITED STATES

One country that many people believe has a legal system that leads to unjust consequences is the United States of America. About 1 in every 20 people in the world live in America. However, about 1 in every 4 prisoners in the world live in America. As America sends so many people to prison, we would hope that their legal system was just and fair. However, this doesn't seem to be the case.

People who have studied the subject have found that if a black person and a white person are accused of the same crime in the U.S.A., the black person is six times more likely to go to prison than the white person. On top of this, black people will probably have to stay in prison for 20% longer than white people for doing exactly the same crime. Many people agree that this shows that the legal system in America is not just or fair because it doesn't treat people equally.

POL POT

Other times, consequences are unjust because they do not punish people enough. Pol Pot was the leader of a government called the Khmer Rouge. The Khmer Rouge took control of Cambodia, a country in Southeast Asia, in 1975 and stayed in power until 1979. During this time, Pol Pot committed genocide and killed over one million people living in Cambodia. 'Genocide' is when huge groups of people are killed because of some characteristic that they all share – usually they have the same **ethnicity**. The main group of people killed by the Khmer Rouge were intelligent and educated people. These people either starved to death, died from being overworked or were simply **executed**.

The flag of Cambodia

The Khmer Rouge held people prisoner and forced them to live and work in horrible conditions.

Although Pol Pot was accused and put on trial for these crimes, he was only placed under house arrest. This meant that he was kept as a prisoner in his own home rather than in a prison. Many people don't think that this was enough punishment for Pol Pot, especially when people in America can go to prison for a long time for only small crimes.

JUSTICE TODAY

There is more justice and equality in the world today than ever before. While no country has a perfect legal system, all countries have some sort of legal system that is designed to help people and bring about justice. However, there are still questions about justice that have not been answered.

JUSTICE FOR CHILDREN

One of the biggest debates relating to justice is about how the law should affect children. Most people would agree that if an adult took sweets from a shop without paying for them, then they should be punished. Most people also agree that if a baby took chocolate from a shop without paying for it, they should not be punished – at least, not by going to court or being sent to prison. This is because babies do not yet understand what is right and what is wrong, whereas an adult usually knows that they should not steal things.

However, at what age do we start saying that the baby can be punished for stealing? 3 years old? 10 years old? 17 years old? This is a very important question and one that a lot of people do not agree on.

CAPITAL PUNISHMENT

Probably the biggest debate concerning justice is whether capital punishment can ever be just. If a person receives capital punishment, it means that they are killed. This is why capital punishment is also called the death penalty.

Today, there are over 50 countries where capital punishment is legal, including the U.S.A., India, Japan and China. In these countries you can legally be killed if you commit serious crimes that are seen as extremely immoral.

- ■ Capital punishment is legal, but hasn't been used in the last ten years
- ▨ Capital punishment is illegal, except for in very special circumstances
- ▨ Capital punishment is illegal
- ■ Capital punishment is legal

This map shows where capital punishment is legal and where it is illegal.

In some parts of the world, however, capital punishment has almost completely disappeared. This is because a lot of people believe that you can never deserve to be killed, no matter how many bad things you do. Only one country in Europe, Belarus, still uses capital punishment and it is not used very often. Less than 20 people have received capital punishment in Belarus in the last 10 years, which does not seem too bad when you compare it to Iran, where over 900 people received the death penalty in 2015 alone.

The death penalty has been used for thousands of years, but many people still do not agree on whether it can ever be a just form of punishment.

CLASS DISCUSSIONS

Do you think that capital punishment can ever be just?

At what age should people start to be punished for things like stealing? Why?

3 What age are you? Can you explain why stealing is wrong?

GLOSSARY

accused	charged with committing a crime or doing something wrong
community	a group of people who live and work in the same area
consequence	the result or effect of an action
court	a group of people who decide whether a crime has been committed
crime	an action or set of actions that break the law
equally	in a manner that is equal
ethnicity	a group of people who share the same nationality and culture
executed	when a person is killed because they were sentenced to death by law or a government
fine	a punishment where one must pay a sum of money
freedom	the power to act, speak, think and live as one wants to
government	the group of people with the authority to run a country and decide its laws
guilty	responsible for a specific immoral action
illegal	forbidden by law
immoral	going against the standard view of what is good and moral
legally	performed within the limits of the law
liberty	being free within society
moral	relating to what is believed to be right or good by a person, group or society
peacefully	without disturbance, violence or war
public	ordinary people in the community
society	a large group of people living together in ordered communities
state	a government and the community that they represent
stela	an upright stone slab or column with some sort of carving on it
symbol	a thing that represents something else, usually a physical object that represents something non-physical
trial	a meeting in court to decide the guilt or innocence of a person or group of people
victims	people who are harmed as the result of crime

INDEX